I Have Wi-Fi to GOD

All Five Bars Rockin'!

I0081104

*One woman's story of neglect, abuse,
and — thanks to an always-present God —
survival and joy.*

By Rose Lauchart
with Reji Laberje

The hope and grace that flows from Rose's story is truly incredible.

Be forewarned that the emotions Rose's story generate may cause your soul to actually ache. Fortunately there is a very different impact that you will be left with, one that will cause you to marvel and wonder if it can actually be true.

Knowing Rose personally and watching this grace be unfold in her life, I can assure you it is true.

                    -Dr. Guy Conn
                      Senior Pastor
                      Fox River Christian Church

<u>A Prayer for the Pages Ahead</u>

May God turn you into a mighty prayer warrior.

May you discern the enemy's schemes, pray God's promises, and shut down the devil at every turn.

May you hear God's voice and know how to pray specifically for those in need before they ever ask for prayer.

May you have eyes to see the new territory God wants to give you and the faith to walk forward and lay hold of it.

And, tonight, rest in the knowledge that God is strong and He is still on His throne.

~Anonymous

I Have Wi-Fi to God – All Five Bars Rockin'!
Author: Rose Lauchart
Contributing Author: Reji Laberje
Editing: Reji Laberje, Griffin Mill
Additional Content Contributions: Jessica Sosnoski
Interior Design: Reji Laberje
Cover Design: Michael Nicloy

Trademark for WFTG AFBR is owned by Rose Lauchart

ISBN-10: 1945907258
ISBN-13: 978-1945907258

BISAC Codes:
FAM001000 FAMILY & RELATIONSHIPS/Abuse/General
REL012120 RELIGION / Christian Life / Spiritual Growth
OCC011020 BODY, MIND & SPIRIT/Healing/Prayer & Spiritual

Published by Nico 11 Publishing & Design
Quantity order requests can be emailed to:
mike@nico11publishing.com

Be well read.

www.nico11publishing.com

<u>Dedication</u>

This story is for all the broken people in the world. If God can fix and mold me, as broken as me and my life were, He can help anyone who lets him.

I want people who read this to have Jesus in their lives and to join the God Warrior army.

Looking for Signals
a prologue

"You will pass through deep waters. But I will be with you. You will pass through the rivers. But their waters will not sweep over you. You will walk through fire. But you will not be burned. The flames will not harm you. I am the Lord your God. I am the Holy One of Israel. I am the one who saves you."

~Isaiah 43:2-3 (NIRV)

Who doesn't hate wandering around in the wilderness? When we're lost, we turn to our devices . . . our phones . . . and we search for connection . . . for a guide . . . for bars raised high. Everything we do today requires those dang bars. We barely even know how to breathe when those bars aren't there . . . when they've been knocked out by people we trusted.

Where do we go then? We don't even know what's in front of us!

Where do we turn when every road we've been on has

detoured us,

stalled us,

and broken us down?

How do we move forward when we don't even know how we got where we are?

How do *I* move forward?

The answer to all of these questions is the easiest thing in the world and also the hardest thing to understand and accept. In order to go forward, we need to go back.

***I* need to go back.**

I need to go back to where we . . . where I . . . had bars . . . and to where they fell down, one-at-a-time, leaving us stranded.

I was stranded.

Today, I tell people I have Wi-Fi to God, but I've been in the wilderness without a connection and I've wandered around without any hope of signaling somebody for help. Nobody wanted me. Nobody loved me. Nobody cared. Experiences and people knocked down my bars; then knocked out my power.

Disregard took down attention.

Abuse took down approval.

Destruction took down growth.

Neglect took down kindness.

But no one could ever take down that fifth bar . . . presence. There was a presence in my life—one that did want me, one that loved me and cared for me; it took decades to recognize the bar that never fell. This is the story of that presence and how, with it, I got all five bars rockin'.

This is my story.

The Bars

Rose Lauchart

Pictures on a Phone
the PRESENCE of God despite difficulty

*"Be strong and courageous. Do not fear or be in dread of them, for it is the L*ORD *your God who goes with you.*
He will not leave you or forsake you."
  ~Deuteronomy 31:6 (ESV)

Rose Lauchart

A gust of chilly Wisconsin autumn wind followed me through the heavy glass door of the tiny writing and publishing company of a small suburban community. This was the place I would be getting naked . . . emotionally speaking, anyway.

"Do you like cats?" I asked the writers, in lieu of *'hello'* as I began this adventure toward creating a memoir of my life. *Adventure* was more their word than mine. I guess that's what they call it when people you trust ask if they can tear open all of your old wounds, pour in a bit of salt and mix it around awhile before cleaning it away and sewing you back up.

"Well, do you? Do you like cats?"

For me, animals have always been a better keeper of my emotions than people ever were. They love you and want only love in return. It's a pretty fair relationship. And dogs and cats don't know how to lie or be something other than what they are, like them or not. You don't have to work too hard to please them . . . just food, water, a roof over their head. They never desire getting high. They don't attack unless threatened. Basic needs are all they want and, in exchange, they provide companionship when you're lonely, compassion when you're sick, and the contentment in simplicity. Around animals, I could just *be* when I didn't want to talk about life; *messy* life . . . made so messy by people who don't have the ability to be honest and authentic like animals do. If people were more like their pets, they would always have all five bars rockin'!

"I have cats. And dogs, too, actually," my new writing partner said.

"We're gonna get along fine," I smiled and we hugged big and tight, something I do openly today.

"You're a hoot!" she says back to me.

Over the next couple of hours, I began giving an overview of the story I was entrusting to people who only knew the cheeky, colorfully-dressed sprite that they described me as. When asked how I know that God is real and I'm connected to him, the answer is simple: "I'm still here, ain't I?" *(By all accounts, I shouldn't be, I think. Killed. Overdosed. Suicide. Any number of toe tags awaited me through the years.)*

I putzed from time to time, with my purposely mismatched silver earrings, wondering if they could see the child who hid beneath the spiky hair and confidence I carried along with me, today. As the questions drew me backward, into my past, my phone gave a chime and I was saved by the bell.

As I shared with friends and neighbors, giving little pieces of what I've been through, I realize that most people wouldn't believe me. It was awful, but it happened; it happened for a reason, maybe. God walked me through valleys, and rocks, and boulders, and cliffs, and—if I could do survive and thrive—so can other people. I need to share with them so that they can figure out their walks and learn, too. There are so many people who need help. They are living as victims because they haven't made the God connection. That's what I have to teach them.

Always one to be connected, I scrolled through my phone to show my new partner the pictures that found their way into the device:

Photos of my cats (of course).

A t-shirt graphic with the letters "WFTG" (Wi-Fi to God).

A quilt I was going to be selling.

A painting of a snowman splattered on a windshield.

Somehow, all of these things would have a place for me as I walked the path of this "adventure" of telling my story.

We moved on through more questions, while my phone beeped and chirped away, a reminder of the many connections I have in my life, today. God has surrounded me with people at church, people I serve with, people who are strong, people who like me for me, people who help me to connect to other positive forces, and people who don't allow me to make negative connections. I wasn't sure I was ready to go back in time to when they weren't there, but that was where we were headed.

"You should know, Rose. This is going to be hard," my biographer said, her hand on mine to offer comfort before we began the journey.

'Hard,' I thought. *'I could do hard.'*

"God told me to tell this story. I'm all in."

The Attention Bar Falls
*the PRESENCE of animals
despite disregard*

*"(God) chose us to be holy
and without blame in his
eyes. He loved us. So he
decided long ago to adopt us.
He adopted us as his children
with all the rights children
have."*

~Ephesians 1:4-5 (NIRV)

Rose Lauchart

was an independent little bitch who wanted to be loved, but nobody wanted me for who I was. It's coarse to say, but it's true. At least it felt true where the people in my life were concerned. I was defiant and didn't want to be in school. I spent most of my pre-schooling years modeling the screaming chaos of my parents' home.

In reality, my independence was just this wall that protected a hurt that was inside of me not getting taken care of. If I was mouthy and brash with grownups or teachers or family, I'd get yelled at . . . but being yelled at was better than not being spoken to at all. I was the little girl who was punished and shamed by her mother for wetting the bed.

Between Kindergarten and First Grade, I slept so soundly that I would wet the bed. Our doctor gave my mother a pad that was attached to an alarm that would train me to wake me in time to get up if it got damp . . . even from sweating. I never slept soundly again. I never had deep sleep. I was always tired. I was emotional. I was unable to quickly heal. Decades later, I suffered from

Fibromyalgia based on a lack of rest that was traced back to those early years. In its time, though, the shame of being a bed-wetter was just one more thing that separated me from others. I didn't have friends. My brothers, Allan and Lee (Leroy) didn't include me.

Edith, my mom, expected a little girl and I was a full-on tomboy. She would buy me these pretty little nylon dresses that I couldn't wait to rip off after we got home from church. Yeah. Church is something that we did, believe it or not. We'd all put on our Sunday best, and ritualistically walk through the readings, repeatings, and routines of a relation-less, rules-driven religion. Then, the Sunday best would come off and so would the fake attitudes my family had in front of the church leaders. By denomination, we were Seventh Day Adventists; looking back on our theology in practice, I realize we were Seven Day-a-Week Hypocrites.

Seventh Day Adventists follow a theology based on the fact that God rested on the seventh day of the week: Saturday. Saturday was our day of worship and rest. The teachings are rule-oriented: no drinking, no movies, no dancing, no meat. It was a life under a dome. I once snuck into town to see "Pinocchio" and another time to eat a burger. If the church had discovered either, the threat of me (and possibly my family) being kicked out of the church was a possibility. At the very minimum, I would have suffered a punishment.

When I got out of my dresses after church on Saturdays, I preferred running around bare-chested like my brothers and I did just that until Mom decided I was getting too grown to do so. I like to think Mom wanted to be around more than she was. Maybe she wanted to make me into a "lady". Maybe, though, she just wanted out of our house as much as I did. Whatever the reason, she worked long hours supporting our family while my Dad, Paul, worked at not necessarily odd jobs, but clearly lower pay than what mom made as a nurse. When she *was* home, she was usually asleep. I used to think it was because she was tired from working so much, or even that she might be lazy. Looking back, maybe it was something more. Depression? An escape?

She had four kids, my Mom. The first baby, Gloria Jean, died when she was just five days old. My sister had to be buried in a pauper's grave with no name on the stone because my folks couldn't afford to have the slab carved.

Before my mom passed away, when she was in a nursing home following a stroke, I spoke to an aunt, who knew where my sister was buried. When we discovered where she was, and got a hold of her birth and death certificates, I paid to have the stone carved with the name "Gloria Jean". My younger brother and I visited the plot and took a picture of the stone to mom in the nursing home. I think it brought her peace knowing that she could go to be with her first born.

After Gloria died, Mom had my brother, Allan; I was born three years later, followed by my brother, Leroy. Mom returned to school for nursing and our family shuffled back and forth for a few years between poor shacks in the states of Michigan and Illinois, winding up at the latter when I began school.

Financially, we struggled, but it meant that I learned a level of financial management that I still maintain today. I always work to have an income; I don't go into debt; I budget, and I can survive on very little. Growing up, vacations were rare and typically meant an army tent that we could pop up on a free piece of property with my parents, brothers, and an uncle from my mom's side who — as a result of the generational gaps created in the mixed blend of large families — was just a couple years older than me and more like a brother. We had some surplus food from the government and that helped us get by, but it was a good thing if you got an orange and a shirt for Christmas. I remember how excited I was one time when Mom got me a t-shirt, like the boys, instead of a dress. It had stripes, was very colorful, and was made of a soft cotton. If I could dress like the boys, maybe I would fit in with them! I felt as though, with that gift, my mom liked me for the kind of girl I was. When I look today at the picture of my Wi-Fi to God t-shirt in my phone, I reflect on its bright colors and how my first t-shirt made me feel accepted.

The men of the family (from both sides) liked to live hard. My brothers, my dad, the three uncles from my mother's side, and two uncles from my dad's side; there was something going on with all of them, particularly when they spent time together on my grandpa's (from my mother's side) property, but I was too young to understand what it might be. I only knew that I wasn't included. My time would come to be loved by the men in my life . . . much sooner than I would have hoped.

I knew that my dad loved me because my mom told me so. When she worked, he was the one to take us to and from school and, later in life, our classmates, too. But, I wasn't really close with all the boys of the family as a young girl. I was a bit of a free-range child, left to my own devices and discoveries.

Then, in first grade, I made my first friend. I played with Frannie, the little girl next door, and she loved me and became, really, the only friend I would ever have in all of my school years. She was gentle, with blonde hair, and this tiny little frail body; I didn't understand just how frail. Her parents loved her (and *me* by extension). Frannie and I played with her small dressing table, and we dreamt of what we would be when we grew up. I often wonder what might have been if she had been able to remain in my life as I grew. I spent every precious, fleeting day with the little girl next door, until one day, she was gone. She lost her battle with leukemia, and she became the first death I understood. My mother never held me to comfort me after I lost Frannie and that felt like second loss to me. Frannie's parents gave me the small dressing table we used to dream over, but I didn't want to play with it alone. Mom tried to give me dolls to play with, but I really just wanted *her* time and *her* touch.

Eventually, Mom gave up trying to give me dolls, but that didn't mean there was newfound time available for me. She decided I could have a real animal. She got some guinea pigs for me and — from that moment on — I had some sort of pet or stray with me throughout the remainder of my childhood. Loving animals and caring for them gave me my fulfillment. With my furry creatures, I always had someone who I felt comfortable with and who accepted me for who I was and what I loved to do and be.

Each one of my animals over the years was full of joy upon seeing me, brought me comfort when I needed affection, and I was safe around them. They would not push me away or forget about me, and I wouldn't forget about them or push them away. We needed each other. I even got my school picture taken with one of my guinea pigs named Billy. He was wonderful. At night, I would say *'It's time for bed,'* and he would walk down the hall, turn left, and wait by my door. He even slept with me. He was a great buddy.

Thought, care, consideration, notice, and awareness are all words used to define attention and they are all things that, as a young girl, I longed for deeply.

I wanted SOMEONE to think of me and the time I needed.

I wanted SOMEONE to care for my feelings of being left out and to offer me love.

I wanted SOMEONE to take a little girl into consideration when planning family activities.

I wanted SOMEONE to notice . . . *me.*

From the people in my life, I got disregard, instead – ignored by brothers, left out of the boys' club of my father and the rest of my male family, and pushed away by my mother. It was as though I had a dirtiness around me, filthy water rising up slowly to envelop me. I was losing any sense of connection . . . of being.

It was only from the animals in my life—everything from guinea pigs, to a dog, to rabbits, to cats over the years—that I found the attention I sought. It's why they make me smile even today as I pass their pictures in my phone. Even in the midst of moving throughout my youth, there always managed to be animals for me to love. It was this comforting presence that found its way to me across the miles and years of my childhood. Sometimes, they literally came to me from afar . . . a stray that seemed to seek me out, directly, as though it was meant for me. I never sought the animals; they found me and, through them, I found my sense of connection and being. With *animals*, I actually felt . . . *human*.

After Frannie, I decided that I didn't belong in school. I didn't fit in. Maybe, just like being the girl in the midst of the boys, I didn't deserve the friendship of classmates. I was so introverted that I didn't talk to anybody. All my own thoughts swirled around in my head clearer than crystal, but getting them out of my head was too much work.

I didn't have anybody—any *people*—that I was comfortable with. Everyone tried to get me to be like them or do what they wanted to do. Why would I feel comfortable just relaxing and being myself with them when it had been made clear to me my whole life that no one wanted that? The boys in my family didn't want me because I was a girl. My mom didn't want me because I wasn't *enough* of a girl . . . and Frannie left me. There were moments in the years to come that I'd wished it had been me.

I didn't have to worry long about schoolmates, though. Just about every other year, we'd move again between different small towns of the two Midwestern states where I was raised. I always wondered why we didn't stay any one place for too long, but as long as I had my animals, I would be okay.

The Approval Bar Falls

the PRESENCE of survival despite abuse

"(God) rescues you from hidden traps, shields you from deadly hazards. His huge outstretched arms protect you – under them you're perfectly safe; his arms fend off all harm. Fear nothing – not wild wolves in the night, not flying arrows in the day, not disease that prowls through the darkness, not disaster that erupts at high noon."

~Psalms 91:1-7 (MSG)

Rose Lauchart

was in the third grade at our church's school. I was sent off to public school after a very short portion of my third grade because I punched a teacher. I had started in a one-room school, and I wanted to either play with my toy car or be allowed to go ahead in my book as I had finished the necessary work. The teacher wouldn't let me do either, so I ripped my book in half and punched her. Based on the model of my older brother as a student, at this point, I was pretty sure this was an appropriate response to frustration or anger; I'd had the chance to see years of verbal fighting between my family members and I just assumed that's how all families were (and that's how all people were).

It was very hard to go from my family's Seventh Day Adventist School into a larger class. In the one-room school, we had grades one through eight, all with children from or connected to the church; there were no more than twenty of us total in the whole school. When it came to academics, church teachings (and rule-based theology) took center stage. Being younger in the one-room school, though, I would often listen to the older students and learn from their lessons.

After my outburst, we were all asked to leave. My older brother would be jumping straight into middle school; I was thrown into an atmosphere of twenty fellow third graders. I wasn't challenged. I wanted to work ahead to be alongside the older students and I couldn't do that. My younger brother, Leroy, was kind of like a light beneath all the mess. He adjusted well.

I, on the other hand, was not good at putting myself out there. I had no idea who these other kids were or how to fit in. It was traumatic for me and I didn't have anyone there to hold my hand or walk me through the new and different practices of this kind of school. From my third grade perspective, my world had just exploded. Even from such a young age, I escaped the institutional walls as often as I could. Since school became more of an occasional hobby, I was glad when my brother, Allan, who was in the sixth grade at the time, decided to start including me.

I was eight-years old when Allan had gotten into a fight and was all revved up and angry. The fight at his new middle school was quite bad. He had broken a tooth and gotten a concussion. In those days, concussions weren't often diagnosed, so the fact that the doctors thought it was a big deal . . . made it into an actually *really* big deal. As I reflect back, I don't think Allan was ever the same after that day.

It was then, following that fight, that Allan first invited me, in the same way he would for the next three and a half years: "Come on. Let's go."

My brother wanted to be with ME! That's all I knew. For the first time, I wasn't going to be ignored, crushed out in this avalanche of being born between the boys. When clothing came off and touching began, I had a funny feeling, wondering, *'Is this right?'*, but I was a kid whose mom was either working, or—from the exhaustion of work—sleeping, and whose dad wasn't around to hang with "the girl". I didn't know I should fear my brother or the moment he'd brought me to. I didn't even know it was abuse. It was the most attention Allan had ever given me. It was the most attention anyone in my family had ever given me.

The memories make a sort of whirlpool in my head; the water clouded with disbelief and foggy recollection of the details. The first time was so emotionally overwhelming that it overshadowed the physical pain. Allan was so much bigger than I. I was there for him because that's what he wanted and I guess I felt like that was what I should do. I didn't know how to stop it or if I should.

After the first time, Allan's invitation would continue fairly regularly and I didn't fight him because I thought this was love and this was normal and this was, above all else, okay and maybe even something I deserved.

The time when I was first abused, I was so young I didn't really know what was going on. I certainly didn't realize I was losing something, because I didn't know any better. *I.*

> *JUST.*

> *DIDN'T.*

> *KNOW.*

If I had known, who could I have told?

I had no trusted adult as a third grade girl who had upset all non-parental authority in my life. I didn't know which men were safe. I had a mother who never offered to help, even with the death of my only friend. I had no peers.

I just dealt with Allan, because it was mine, much like losing Frannie. The pain was mine. The confusion was mine. It was all mine and there wasn't anybody there that I thought would listen to me and join in, soothe, or protect me from my brother.

Back then, there weren't any resources about this sort of thing. They didn't teach "appropriate touching" in school or youth groups and organizations; people weren't talking about this kind of stuff . . . certainly not to poor girls with no roots and no community. I let it eat me up inside, always a bit unsure if my instincts about right and wrong were correct. I didn't think I had any choice about it being any other way.

In the midst of the abuse, when I was ten years old, my brother grabbed a rifle and shot through the floor at my feet. It didn't harm me, but it let me know that he was capable of pulling the trigger. It was a show of power. That's what he was about.

It was always pretty much the same whenever Allan wanted something . . .

wanted it . . . wanted me. He'd say, "Come on. Let's go," and I followed in obligation.

So what *was* going on with the men in my family? Uncles, brothers, parents, generations of rapists and perpetrators of incest and molestation of boys, girls, women, children; it didn't matter what gender or age. It was abuse of that unmentionable kind . . . sexual crimes being committed by individuals, each outdoing the others in his perversion.

There was a semi-trailer on my grandpa's property and one of my teenage uncles would meet grade school boys there. My older brother and youngest uncle had to witness the acts. Eventually, Allan had learned enough that he could take part in them. I'm not sure how old he was at that time and wonder still how much of a victim he had been before he became the villain. Two of my five uncles were so predatory, that they would go to extremes to fulfill their dark lust. One uncle was forbidden from alone time with me or any female, and had a wife who lived in fear of parents knocking on her door with news of his abuses on their daughters. Another uncle would physically harm himself to be able to have access to female nurses. Their professional touches were gropes of pleasure in his twisted mind. This was the same uncle who one day abused his own granddaughter. Even as a young girl, his gaze made me feel naked. I ended up learning that it was not uncommon for my dad's brother to have sex with his sisters when they were growing up. Not all of these secrets were revealed at once; rather, each passage of time lent itself to more filth being discovered. I felt the scum rising around me like mud, making it hard to move and giving me the sensation of being stuck.

In those early days on my grandpa's property, older teens, sometimes including my own brother, would bring in the young boys to be taken by the older boys. This legacy of twisted scandal was kept alive on both sides of the family: women who didn't stand up for themselves or save their daughters from the rapes, men who did not raise their sons to learn that this was unacceptable and vile behavior, and families that were kept from talking and kept on moving so that they wouldn't get caught for the heinous acts. They hid from the truth because it was easier to do nothing than to risk the shame (especially in front of the church) of dealing with the culture of the families.

I learned the truth about all of the men in my life. All of them but my own father and younger brother were a part of this loveless legion of predators and pedophiles.

I was the little girl . . . the only girl . . . suffering at the hands of it.

I was seeking approval from those who never asked for mine. Family members who sought such approval from the men in their lives received punishment in the form of incest and self-loathing. It was an abuse no child (or person) should ever have to understand. I'd already dreaded school for years, but now I hated nights and the weekends as well, because there was no escape from my tormentor or this new reality of my childhood existence. It took several years before I finally had the answer to my eight-year-old wondering:

"NO! No, this isn't right. No."

When we moved back to Illinois when I was in the sixth grade, I decided I wouldn't submit to my brother anymore. *I was going to be the first woman to break loose.*

I was fighting with Allan one day. I'm sure in my head and heart that the fight was about my realization of his evil acts more than the moment we were in at that time. We were screaming and throwing things. I don't remember how it started, really, but it got pretty rough and I remember how it ended. I had one of those metal choker chains for dogs and all of the *'Come on. Let's go.'* invitations from the last three years boiled up inside of me. I held onto that chain, threw it hard, and hit him on the side of the head with the choker. He was dazed and he was bleeding, and he lost it; he literally lost it and — for the first time — I knew enough to be afraid. In a moment, half a breath, a skipped heartbeat, I went into self-preservation mode.

I ran and locked myself in the bathroom in a desperate effort to simply stay alive. I was in fear for my life and knew that if Allan got a hold of me, he'd strangle me. I was in limbo behind that bathroom door, caught between life and death. The dog was at the door, but I didn't know who was going to lead him away and cage him. My brother, the raging mad dog was going to do something to me if he caught me.

Allan's temper had been known to rock the whole tiny house we lived in. He would yell and scream, slam things, and even foam at the mouth with fury in those times when he could not express himself or get his way. My brother was completely out of control when he was angry. I remember that look he would get in his eyes, on his face, and in the posturing of his whole body, when you knew something was about to set him off in a fury. He would turn into someone else, some*thing* else; it was monstrous. I was frightened of those moments, but—finally— I was disgusted enough with myself for being his slave (for so long) that I *became* the thing that set him off.

I don't even know what happened next, but I thankfully hadn't been alone in the house. Somehow, whoever was at home with us managed to get Allan out of the house so they could then get me out . . . and get both of us to protection from one another for awhile.

There was no reason I should have survived that day. My brother was so out of control, he could have killed me before I ever decided to hit him. After I hit him, there was no reason he shouldn't have reacted more quickly; he was ruthless when he was raging. When I ran, there was no reason he shouldn't have caught me as his size, strength, and age were those of a young man. While I hid in that bathroom, there was no reason someone should have come to my rescue before Allan managed to break down the door. I don't know where the strength came from to say, "No," and I sure as hell don't know how that "No" turned out to be the last time Allan would touch me in madness or molestation. It's like I was tapped into something greater than myself and I used that to lean in to my first escape.

Allan and I were taken from the home for a couple of weeks and my brother never came back. He had a sort of foster family situation from that day until he left for the Marine Corps and, while living with them, he also got engaged, so he had disconnected somewhat from his birth family. In the years before he graduated, we went to the same schools, but didn't speak to one another and weren't left alone together. We tried to make amends verbally before he left for the Marines, but he never said he was sorry; he never admitted that what he did was wrong; and he never asked me how I was.

We shared a few letters after Allan shipped off to the war in Vietnam because that was the things I felt should happen with servicemen. This was my brother, after all. We might have found peace, one day; I'd like to think so, anyway, but Allan only came home from Vietnam in the form of a name on a wall. You will find the eternal eighteen year-old, PFC Allan David Timmerman, on panel E2 of the Vietnam War Memorial, today.

In the immediate aftermath of Allan being gone from the house and me being back in my parents' home, though, I thought my abuse was over. It would be a few more years before he joined the military, but he was away from me, so I had to be safe, right? I wish that feeling had lasted.

I was lying down for a rest on my parent's bed one day to get cool, an undeveloped girl of eleven years old. I was just in panties because it was such a hot day. My father came into the room, and I froze, pretending to be asleep, hoping my father would go back out. I hoped in that moment that my dad was different. He wasn't. He approached the bed; he placed his finger into the waistband of my underwear, and he pulled down to look at what was underneath. My heart pounded with such terror that I couldn't move; I couldn't call for help; I couldn't open my eyes to show him I was really awake. Then, he left.

To this day, I don't know why he left me lying there alone. I've learned enough about the men in my life that I recognize it wasn't his own power holding him back. It was one more lost connection in a life that longed for exactly that sensation.

The fact that my father could ever think to do such a thing messed with me even more than the years of Allan's abuse. On that day when my eyes were closed with my Dad, I opened my eyes to other things that I somehow didn't see before. The classmates my dad had been driving home? Young girls like me . . . sixth and seventh graders? He would meet them out alone. My father had been going through my little address book that I was so proud to begin building with names of real people. All along, I was just building a list of new victims. It was one of the biggest abuses of all, making me into a party to the perpetrators.

I never saw it, not imagining my Dad had in him the same sickness of my brother and so many of my uncles. It was traumatic and forever remained on my mind and conscience. I lost all respect and all trust of, not just my father, but all men that day and for most of the rest of my life.

The filth around me was suffocating and connection waned. If attention and approval were bars I could climb to wholeness, I was lost forever.

◈

Time marched on, lost without connection . . .

There was a family that lived next door to us – a husband, a wife, and five kids. The wife was a piece of work. She was sleeping with a truck driver . . . who was not her husband. The truck driver was living at the house with them, and then she would go on the road with him. At some point they let me go with them, mostly to cover their tracks, as though she was going along to look after me and I was the one who wanted to join this truck driver. We stopped at a truck stop and saw this great, big, huge, stuffed panda bear. I so dearly wanted it, so they got it for me as a thirteenth birthday gift. They also had a friend; I don't know how old he was, but I knew I was way too young to be going out with him. When you have low self-esteem, any attention is better than no attention. I was allowed to go out with this guy, and he was having sex with me; protected sex, thank God, because it could have been a problem. I thought it was love. I literally knit this guy a sweater for Christmas, so desperate to be able to show love and affection in the same way I yearned to feel it in return.

❧ ❧

Time marched on, lost without connection . . .

When I was in eighth grade, my appendix nearly burst. After I had it taken out, my mother said, "I want you to go where I went to high school."

It was a Seventh Day Adventist, live-in, boarding school. Mom bought me all sorts of new things and took me away to Michigan. Maybe she was trying to help me in her own way, but, once again, help was outsourced to someone else or something else. Within six weeks of my being at the new school, the woman who was in charge of the female dorm told me I had broken all the rules that it took most girls four years to break.

They had prayer meeting every night, which I skipped. I was downstairs in the laundry room with one of my friends dying my hair black . . . and I'd had strawberry blonde hair. The next day I went to class, and the teacher freaked, because you're not supposed to dye your hair. He said "you dyed your hair." I said "Yep." He said "Guess what? You're done in class until you dye it back." I said, "OK I'll see you" and I didn't go back to class. I'd snuck into town to eat (meat, of all things). I'd gone to a movie. It may not sound like much, but it was rebellious in that environment.

I was expected to go to school half a day and work half a day. Because they couldn't find me a job, they stuck me on duty at the campus laundry. I called my mom and said "Here's the deal, Mom. I can't go back to class, because I dyed my hair. I'm not learning anything working, because the job stinks. I'm sitting here spending your money and eating. You decide. You wanna have me stay here and pay for it, or you wanna come get me?"

It took a couple of those phone calls before she finally gave in to come bring me home. Maybe it was Stockholm Syndrome, but as bad as home was, I knew how things worked there and didn't want to be away from it.

⤶⤷

Time marched on, lost without connection . . .

When I came home from the boarding school I was in the middle of the ninth grade. I was able to get a babysitting job through the hospital. In the summer I finished enough credits to start as a sophomore and that's how I began my high school career. That lasted two weeks. It just wasn't me. I got on the bus, rode to school, and I would walk home after homeroom, which was a couple of miles. Finally I thought, *'well that's real stupid, why don't you just stay home instead of walking home all those miles after taking the bus?'* I couldn't do anything about it, yet, but the musings of a future dropout began.

There are different ways to learn, and they didn't know that then. I was stuck in the cracks. Had I gotten the right guidance when I was younger, I could have had a lucrative career, because I'm not stupid. I didn't. It just wasn't meant to be. I'm meant to be a God warrior, so here I am.

When I was fifteen years old, my little brother and I were walking home from a movie. We only lived ten blocks from town . . . about a mile, we weren't old enough to drive. On the way home, a car pulled up beside us. One of the two guys inside asked, "Want a ride?" I said "Well I just live down a couple blocks." He said "I don't care, I asked if you want a ride." I said "OK sure." I got in the car. My brother said he would be telling my mother, but I didn't care. I sensed the intentions of the guy weren't clean. After all, he didn't ask if Leroy wanted a ride. Nonetheless, feeling rebellious, looking for danger, and taking risks were all things that could lead to the approval and connection I sought.

I became a statistic . . . pregnant at age fifteen. I got pregnant on January 2nd, though I didn't know it until later. I would have other news before then. I didn't tell the father, much to my parents' disapproval, until they convinced me to take him to court for child support and medical expenses. I barely knew or had an actual relationship with him, though. I received minimal child support from him, and he got some visitation rights. He eventually stopped showing up for his visits, and since my son was about 10, has been completely out of contact with him.

❧❧

Time marched on, lost without connection . . .

I dropped out of school before I even knew I was pregnant. My mother called the administration and told them, "Well, here's the deal. In three weeks, Rose is gonna be sixteen and she's gonna quit."

They told her I should bring my books in when I *was* sixteen. Knowing that they were probably going to try to talk me out of it, I took my books across the street to a neighbor, instead, and told them to take them in for me. I wasn't going back. I was done. I didn't go back to school and it was ten years before I got my GED.

❧ ❧

Time marched on, lost without connection . . .

News from the government: Allan was killed in Vietnam on January 12th, 1967.

Finding out that I was pregnant, shortly after Allan's death, took on new meaning. I would never get peace with my older brother. I would never be accepted by Allan or loved by him. Suddenly, this child growing inside of me became my personal attempt at finding someone of my very own to love and cherish. It would be someone who would love me unconditionally in return, too.

Until I had the gift of my son in my life, though, it was time for the family to wait for Allan's remains to be shipped home for burial. An uncle came and stayed with us while we waited. At times, my parents left us in the home alone. That's when his advances began. Knowing that I was almost done with this life, I didn't even fight him when he was on top of me. Sex with the married man, another bit of filth from my family, was meaningless. Better things were ahead if I could just get past the moment.

❧

Time marched on, lost without connection . . .

I tried to bond with Allan's fiancée and even slept at her place for a while, but I learned the common bond she shared with Allan: *violence*. In a fit of anger one day, she pulled a gun while I slept and shot. She missed my body by an inch. The cord with my brother had truly been cut.

❧

Time marched on, lost without connection . . .

My dad didn't speak to me at all throughout my pregnancy. I had my son, Rob, when I was sixteen. I tried to raise him, but it didn't feel as I thought it would. He cried and required exhaustive attention. He didn't cling to me and love me as I imagined he would from the start. He was just a baby, but so was I. I didn't understand that emotional connections develop over time. It felt, instead, that even the boy I had grown inside of me was rejecting me. I didn't know how to be a mother and the void inside of me remained empty.

At some point, I brushed against a cigarette and accidentally burned my arm. I realized it felt good to hurt myself . . . to feel something. I held the cigarette firmly against my arm and burned myself deeper; I still have the scar. The physical pain took away from my emotional pain.

Eventually, I would cut myself, too, just to watch the bleeding. It was never too deep —just enough to feel. I'd pull down the sleeves of long-sleeved shirts over the markings, hiding the physical pain from the world in much the way nobody could see my emotional mess. Like so many instances from my youth, it was one more thing that was just for me. Nobody knew and there was no consequence. It was something in my life that I controlled.

None of it helped ease my drowning, though. My new escape became drugs; a mix of uppers and downers. The uppers helped me put on my tough façade through the two jobs and flirtatious manner I kept; the downers helped me sleep peacefully through the night.

Eventually, I met Bruce. I believed he was the man who would take me to my next chapter in life and maybe even a man who loved me (as well as I could fathom love).

Rob was about three when I was ready to move out of my parents house. I told him he could either go with me, or stay with Grandma and he chose to stay with Grandma. Part of me thought that my parents would love him more than they ever could have loved me. He wouldn't be hurt in the way I had been. He wouldn't experience the rising tide of scum enveloping his soul. I could never be the girl my family wanted, but I could finally be a woman they could be proud of, by bringing a child to them. What greater proof of womanhood than bearing a child; a son? I would leave Rob behind with the family that I'd waited nineteen years to either escape, or be embraced by. For me, it would be escape; for Rob, I hoped it would be an embrace.

My childhood was over.

<u>The Growth Bar Falls</u>
the PRESENCE of truth
despite denial

"...I don't mean to say that I have already achieved these things or that I have already reached perfection. But I press on to possess that perfection for which Christ Jesus first possessed me. No, dear brothers and sisters, I have not achieved it,[a] but I focus on this one thing: Forgetting the past and looking forward to what lies ahead, I press on to reach the end of the race and receive the heavenly prize for which God, through Christ Jesus, is calling us."

~Philippians 3:12-14 (NLT)

Rose Lauchart

When I dropped out of school, I went and got myself a job, because the positive parts of adult life that I recognized were all about working and making money. I started in a restaurant, A&W, because I was too young to work anywhere else. When I got my driver's license and I was old enough, I went to work at a plastics factory, but I also kept my A&W job as a car hop. I ultimately ended up managing the whole place.

I lived off the A&W money, and I saved up my factory money to buy my own car, a brand new 1970 baby blue Plymouth Barracuda convertible (that I still wish I had). I think about that car and it reminds me of when my brother Lee taught me how to drive a stick-shift car. Lee and I never had much of a relationship as we both ignored the life we had to live through; but time learning with him is a good memory and, being one of few, I still treasure it to this day.

By day, I was at the restaurant, and — by night — at the plastics factory.

I met Bruce while he was still married, though no longer living with his soon-to-be ex-wife. The cost of divorce had kept them from finishing the proceedings. Despite his own drug and alcohol use, he helped me to get clean. I saw the world clearly for the first time in a few years. Because of this ironic beginning, I thought he cared for me on a different level than any man ever had. I helped pay for his divorce, bought my first home, and Bruce moved in with me. It was a mobile home on a rented lot, the only thing I could afford at that time. Marriage followed shortly afterward and it seemed my life might have some semblance of normalcy. Rob visited only occasionally and Bruce referred to him as Robbie Hayseed; it *wasn't* a compliment.

Bruce's alcohol and cocaine use didn't bother me. I'd been more frightened by men who never touched either. Every night while I worked, Bruce worked the bars, drinking like a fish and hustling pool. I found out that he had a reputation for being a mean drunk. In his past, he had beaten one of his "loves" half senseless. One night, I'd gotten off of work at 11:00 P.M. and had gone to sleep, exhausted from work. He came in hours later, after the bars closed and took advantage of my sleeping body. I awoke to him raping me.

If I spent money, we fought. If he thought somebody was looking at me in clothes that made me feel beautiful, we fought, (and he made me wear different clothing; he even made me wear these big glasses that I didn't like because he thought they made me less attractive). He never hit me. Our fights were mostly just yelling, swearing, putting me down, accusing me of the acts that he was guilty of committing (drugs, going to bars, and even adultery), and his showing of control, power, or authority. I was his property and his income, though he was never mine.

We'd been married about seven years when we were having a big fight; Bruce pulled a rifle out and said, "You want to see me shoot you?" It was just a sick joke to him, but, "No!" I screamed and I walked out. We never spoke about the incident.

Shortly after his gun "joke", I was going through the normal stresses of work, and experiencing maternal stress as my parents looked after my son (a combination of guilt, and an inability to cope); I was in full-fledged emotional upheaval. I didn't know what was real and what wasn't real anymore. I was visiting a colleague's house and she had a plant on the table. I asked if I could get a cutting of it; *it was a plastic plant*, and not the kind that would pass for living. My world had become a series of mirages and fake fronts to the point that I didn't even know a real plant anymore. I checked myself into a mental hospital. At the time, it felt like an escape, but—while there—I was diagnosed with "Anxiety Disorder with a Near Complete Breakdown." I never even understood the difference between want and need . . . right and wrong. I mean I really hadn't learned these things. Ever. I learned more in those ten weeks than ever in my life.

I got into crafting and art when I was at the hospital and discovered that I had an ability to create beautiful things. I would eventually tap into the art of quilting, which felt appropriate, piecing together a collection of mismatched bits to make something whole and new. Crafting, painting, and sewing: they became new kinds of escapes that were far healthier than sex, work, or drugs. I wouldn't truly recognize this gift for many years.

Today, I look at the many quilts I've created as I scroll through my phone, and I see more than their eventual owners ever will.

I see the many broken bits that were put into each square.

I see the changing dimensions of reality in the different shapes.

I see the attempts at wholeness.

I see the hope for beauty in the mismatched patterns and colors.

I see . . . *myself.*

The hospital was constant control and questioning. It felt to me like they were lying while the world I thought I understood changed beneath me. It was the first time I realized that my childhood hadn't been normal, that my treatment had been abuse. They tried to teach me tools that I wasn't connecting with, things that would help me recognize my own dangerous situations, but it was all so foreign to me, like reading about a different world in a story. The world that I was learning about was so different from the one I had built around myself; and I was afraid of it.

After my time in the hospital, trying to absorb the strange lessons I'd learned, I felt I was ready to check back into the world.

Bruce would mess with me at home, putting me down for having lost it. He played head games with me, telling me he tossed my wedding ring when I was away (while I was wearing it), so that I might think I was simply *imagining* a ring. He fashioned extension cords into two male ends just to mess with my mind. It was funny to him that I had lost it.

Never sure if I really had it together, I numbly moved back into a routine of going through the self-destructive motions with Bruce. We would last another six years that way. I continued working, now at the factory and, over my lunch breaks, as a Go-Go dancer at restaurants and bars. The pay was good and kept Bruce satisfied. He drank and did drugs, spending my money, but he didn't threaten me, anymore.

Sometimes, we'd even connect, like when we rode our motorcycles to Sturgis one year for the famous annual bike rally. This was an activity we shared with my friend, Spencer. The following year, Spencer asked us to a rendezvous camping trip in Custer Park in South Dakota over Labor Day Weekend. We drove out there in Spencer's semi, then, at his home, we packed up his teepee and family, and went to Custer State Park for the long holiday weekend event. We met and had good time, together, but Bruce didn't want the fun to end. When it came time to go home, I returned to work, and Bruce went west with Spencer, to help him deliver his semi loads of various merchandise.

Over the course of the next *six weeks*, I heard from Bruce only when he wanted me to send money. I realized, with Bruce gone, that—for the first time in my life—I was alone. I felt far less stressed with him gone, but also lonely, still tapping into that inner child who longed for attention. I told Bruce we were over. I don't know if I would have had the ability to do so without him having left.

I realized that, while I had set out on my own to grow as an adult, I had spent the last thirteen years of my life in stagnant water. The players had changed, but I had not. I was still stuck in filth . . . still drowning.

Then, and maybe the reasons weren't right, just as my reasons weren't right when I was a pregnant teenager, but I wanted my son; I wanted Rob back. He was sixteen years old when I invited him to live with me.

He would stay with me (and eventually, my second husband) until he was twenty-three. It wasn't nearly enough time, but I finally got to be with my son.

Rob later shared that he didn't blame me for anything, but the beginning years were kind of like two people who kind of knew each other, but not really, and we were attempting to live together. I did what I thought a mother should do: feed him (he ate like a garbage disposal), meet with his school, encourage him to get a job, and the like.

I tried to instill the lessons I learned in the mental hospital, even though it was still hard for me to believe them myself.

We didn't deserve one another, Rob and me; we both should have had better. I can't make up for the years of my life when I couldn't be the mother he deserved, but I move forward each day trying to be the best mom I can with what I've learned.

The Kindness Bar Falls
the PRESENCE of forgiveness
despite neglect

"Encourage one another and build one another up, just as you are doing."
~1 Thessalonians 5:11
(ESV)

Rose Lauchart

Dan was a first-generation American whose older brother, being the oldest male in a traditional European family, was the recipient of the family's full attention. Dan grew up neglected. His dad called him the wrong name routinely and he was treated as a second class citizen in his own family. While he didn't have to endure the physical abuse I had in my childhood, he was equally disregarded. Neither of us knew *how* to connect in an intimate familial relationship. He had been married years ago for about two years and had one child in that relationship but was cheated on. His wife had been sleeping with his friend while he was away in the military. When he discovered the adultery, he walked away from the marriage.

He lunched at one of the restaurants where I danced and, while Bruce and I were apart, Dan and I began to get to know one another. I'm not sure exactly what it was that was different about him from the other men in my life except that he seemed to respect me, and this was an entirely new concept for me.

When Dan first called me, I met him for a drink and he didn't try to get handsy with me. It was a real date. I realized that, before that time, I hadn't ever been on an actual date; I'd only hooked up with men and, through that, fell into relationships defined by sex.

The first time he saw me, before Bruce and I were divorced, he told the guys he was with, "I'm going to marry her one day."

Dan was safe and—at the same time— he gave me an escape from Bruce. I'm not too proud to admit that I was strengthened toward kicking out Bruce by the safety net that Dan provided. Once my divorce was finalized, I didn't really want to marry again, but I did want somebody with me. Because Dan said he didn't believe in living together outside of marriage, we wed.

Dan had a job, so I didn't think I was going to be used. I didn't wanna lose him because I wasn't ready to be alone. I don't know who I felt I was, but I wasn't well enough, mentally, to be alone. It was only six weeks into the marriage when Dan said he thought our quick marriage was a mistake. I threatened suicide. I don't honestly know if I would have followed through, but in the moment, I thought I want to end my life. We eventually worked it out and he did stay, but I told him I couldn't function unless he made a true, emotional commitment. Dan was more than my love; he was the one in the wings that helped me get out of another mess, and I wasn't ready to give that up . . . to give him up.

Dan was great with Rob. In some ways, though I know it wasn't right, it hurt me. They were like two boys playing together, building bonfires and bonding. I was left out again, like I had been as a little girl. Rob lived with us for about five years before moving away as an adult.

My marriage to Dan felt completely different than marriage between Bruce and I. Dan worked a lot on the railroad, the first man in my life to be such a diligent worker; I worked a lot at the factory; we didn't see one another much. Most of our relationship was on the phone and seeing one another once every week or two.

When we were together, we had good conversations and ate dinner together. I felt like a child, learning this new routine. We didn't agree on much as far as lifestyles or values, but we weren't hurting one another, and that was a step up from our abusive backgrounds.

Dan would call me the few times when I was the one who was away, in utter loneliness. I was supposed to be able to be without him when he was on the railroad, but he couldn't manage even the smallest things without me. We were in a mutually co-dependent relationship, each relying on the other to maintain a specific schedule and routine, the neutral comfort of reliability.

We had a physical relationship, but it was minimal. I was unsure how to be in a sexual relationship without it being drunkenness, rape, or submissive to fear. When we were together, it was out of obligation of the marital relationship. It wasn't abuse, but it also wasn't connection . . . just like the rest of our relationship.

Though alcohol wasn't a driver in the way Dan treated me, it was still a problem. He drank after hours to the point of sometimes not being able to go into work the next day. At times, it was because he was still drunk and other times, because he was hung-over. Driving drunk wasn't an unusual practice, either. I was merely grateful he wasn't a violent alcoholic. He sometimes said verbally abusive things, such as calling me trashy or implying that I was below him, but we didn't discuss them when he was sober, so I wasn't sure if he even remembered them or not. I'd like to think he didn't, or at least that he didn't mean them.

I tried to connect Dan with his own son, but he wasn't ready. About ten or eleven years into the marriage, his son called. He came to visit his dad and we welcomed him. The cycle had continued in his son . . . an absent father, a mother that ultimately had left him with her parents. He didn't know how to connect and he turned to alcohol and drugs to deal with his issues.

The two of them made attempts, though, at building a relationship. They began to speak regularly. We both worked hard and managed to save the money to visit his son (and his family) in Alaska, where they lived. The two men spent time together, but we discovered that he had come to us for money, more than time and attention. We both offered the latter, but it wasn't enough. From the time we got home, each contact became only about money. It was a devastating blow to Dan who longed, as much as I, for human connection and love.

For the first time in my life—maybe because it was the first time I had any of it—money became an issue. I was in charge of the money; it came in and went out. The two of us would both shop to fill emotional holes. I shopped for *stuff* and he bought alcohol, sometimes buying rounds for a whole bar, in order to be the good friend. We both collected things and moments, while still feeling empty.

We were financially drowning and went in for bankruptcy counseling; the cost of the bankruptcy was so high that we couldn't afford to get out of the debt. Irony at its finest. We instead went to credit counseling and found a way to lower, and then make, our regular payments. Then, when Dan's father passed away, we received enough of an inheritance to be able to pay off all of our debt. We worked as a team and it was a triumphant feeling for each of us.

Twelve years into our marriage of comfort, Dan was diagnosed with prostate cancer. He had to have his prostate removed and, even though he superficially looked the same, he was self-conscious as a man. From that time forward, Dan never touched me again. I spent the last sixteen years of my marriage to Dan in a relationship devoid of intimacy. The loss was emotionally crushing to me. From the time I had been just eight years old, the act of sex was what I knew I could bring value to; it may have been wrong, but it was part of my identity and I lost it.

Because Dan felt like he couldn't have sex, he never wanted to push into *anything* that could lead to it. He didn't kiss, hug, or even hold my hand again after his prostate cancer. It was as much my fault as his; I allowed it; we never talked about it. I'd spent most of my life being used for my body and having all physical touch taken away from me made me feel as though I had nothing left to offer.

Dan retired and, with nothing left to fill his time, his spending habits picked back up, probably to fill the voids that still remained and were newly found. We ran our home on a cash budget. On payday, he pulled his full cash for the pay period. He went directly to the bar and spent it in its entirety. One day, too early in the day for decent people to be drinking, I got a call from the local police department that he had been in an accident. I had to pick him up at the accident site.

I told him, "You're done drinking." He never did, again.

Twice, he tested me. One time, he tried to have a bottle of wine opened so that "we" could try it. Another time, he wanted to enjoy a "meal" that was served in a bar. Neither time did I budge. We didn't keep alcohol in the home, anymore, either; alcohol had never been my crutch of choice, so it wasn't a loss to me.

Drinking had been Dan's crutch, though, and—without it—it was like he no longer wanted to try standing at all. He didn't want to take care of himself. Smoking took over for drinking and became an even bigger problem. He had a heart attack that led to stents in his heart. I took away the smoking, but it was too late. The stent in his artery ultimately went sideways and caused even more damage. A pacemaker was put in. It wasn't enough.

Weak from his heart attack and lack of wellness, Dan fell down at home and cut himself. Because he was on blood thinners, he bled everywhere. He went to the hospital where all of his health issues crashed in upon him at once.

I was bitter about the whole situation.

❦❦

Shortly before these final days, I had been driven to return to church. It was an awkward place for me, attending this non-denominational setting where rules were cast aside except for the golden one:

> *"Love the Lord your God with all your heart and with all your soul and with all your mind and with all your strength.' The second is this: 'Love your neighbor as yourself.' There is no commandment greater than these."*
>
> *~Mark 12:31-32 (NIV)*

Relationship replaced rituals in this new place, in teachings, and amongst one another. The church was holding a Valentine's Day event for couples and I convinced Dan to attend.

The whole dinner was for married couples to reconnect, and I thought *'what do*

I have to lose?' I had to take a stab at it, I felt like I owed it to Dan and I to make it work. I really did want it to work and—at this point—I had made him stop drinking. I got the tickets! Between the time we got the tickets and the dinner, he was in and out of the hospital. If dinner had gone as planned, we probably would have returned home and had discussions at least about things we needed to do to get closer together again. But, Dan ate dinner, and after finishing, he said "I'm ready to go home."

The part of the evening we had truly come for was hearing the speaker and learning tools for marriage. I felt cheated because he didn't want to put in the effort to go through with the whole thing. I felt like he was making an ass of me, and I apologized to the table: "I'm sorry, but this is what I have to deal with."

It was embarrassing that I had to be with this guy who didn't even want to make the effort to go into the auditorium and hear the message.

At that point, I don't think I cared what anyone actually thought; I was just plowing through. We left. I think he knew why I was upset. I let him have it in the car. I said "I'm done! I'm not doing this anymore! I'm not driving anywhere with you! I'm not going anywhere with you! I'm done!"

Dan didn't really have a reaction; he just listened. I think I felt liberated after that, but I reflected on the night and realized just how broken our marriage was. I had listened to everybody else's love stories around the table: how they met, what they did for fun, their long-term dreams and goals, and I realized Dan and I didn't have any of it. It felt like my whole marriage was a sham.

When I look back at my picture of my Frost Meets Frosty quilt as I scroll through my phone, I'm brought back to this moment. The painting is of a snowman splattered against a winter windshield, twig arms, coal eyes, and carrot nose all scattered to the ends of the display. Cold collision. That's how my life felt in my moment of realization; that was the day I recognized that I'd spent an entire lifetime without real relationship.

❧ ❧

After Dan fell, I wasn't just bitter about him not taking care of himself. I was angry that we never would be able to have the type of relationship I had learned about on that Valentine's Day. I was angry with him and with myself for not knowing better and for not caring for one another as we both needed.

Dan was going to need to be put into hospice care. His time was coming very soon. Being alone and, given Dan's size and condition, I didn't feel confident that I could care for him at home. I told the nurses that he needed to stay in the hospital for his hospice care and that I wouldn't be able to take care of him alone at home. He was in the hospice for five days after being in the hospital for nearly two weeks, and ultimately, passed away during a time I was not there.

When we had sat together in his hospital room for the last time before he went into hospice care, I looked at him with a newly discovered sadness.

"We weren't very kind to one another, were we?" I asked.

"No. We weren't," he said.

Then, we both apologized to one another and forgave one another for not filling the voids in our separate lives.

We recognized in that moment, that we both deserved better and, in that realization, we made peace with one another.

In hospice, Dan was only awake and functional for about 48 hours. The last three days he was in a coma, and I sat with him as much as I could. I left the hospice to go home to sleep, and got the call the next morning that he had passed.

We had been married twenty-eight years. With Dan's passing, I was alone with myself for the first time in my life.

Rose Lauchart

Disconnected
all bars down

"Do you think anyone is going to be able to drive a wedge between us and Christ's love for us? There is no way! Not trouble, not hard times, not hatred, not hunger, not homelessness, not bullying threats, not backstabbing…None of this fazes us because Jesus loves us…nothing living or dead, angelic or demonic, today or tomorrow, high or low, thinkable or unthinkable – absolutely nothing can *get between us and God's love because of the way that Jesus our Master has embraced us."*

~Romans 8:38-39 (MSG)

Rose Lauchart

Moses wandered around for forty years feeling forgotten by God. I think I can relate to his journey as I moved through the decades of my life feeling like I had yet to make a connection. I kept trying to climb toward a feeling of love and wholeness, but the path kept falling away.

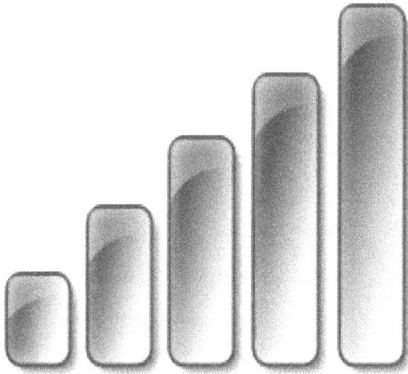

Attention was taken
down by disregard.

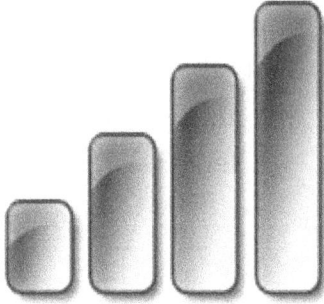

Approval was taken
down by abuse.

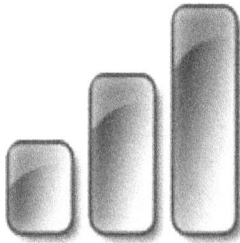

Growth was taken
down by self-destruction.

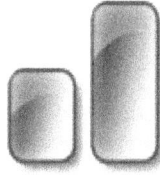

Kindness was taken
down by neglect.

But, one thing never went away. There was a presence that kept me from drowning, even as my soul was enveloped in filth. Something kept me from being enveloped and overwhelmed by the sands of life.

Rose Lauchart

Presence
a never-failing connection

"The Lord is my shepherd; I have what I need. He lets me lie down in green pastures; He leads me beside quiet waters. He renews my life; He leads me along the right paths for his name's sake. Even when I go through the darkest valley, I fear no danger, for you are with me; your rod and your staff — they comfort me... Only goodness and faithful love will pursue me all the days of my life, and I will dwell in the house of the Lord as long as I live."
~Psalm 23 (CSB)

Rose Lauchart

What was it that called me back to church to discover the bar that had kept me going? Several years ago, at a family event, I was standing at the kitchen counter when one of my uncles approached me from behind and kissed my neck. This was my most trusted uncle, my friend, and the man I had seen as a brother.

Suddenly, I was an unloved child who had just lost her best and only friend.

I was ignored by my mother.

I was in third grade, hearing Allan's *'Come on. Let's Go.'*

I was standing firmly while a rifle was fired at my feet.

I was in sixth grade, hiding in fear for my life behind a bathroom door.

I was eleven years old on my parents' bed, pretending to sleep while my father stripped down my panties.

I was a thirteen years old with a wish for a teddy bear and the reality of a grown man.

I was fifteen, sleeping with a stranger who would give me a son.

I was sixteen, mourning the loss of a brother who never said he was sorry while sleeping with an uncle who took out his grief on me in the bed.

I was wondering why another gunshot missed my head.

I was burning my own flesh.

I was cutting into my arms.

I was suicidal.

I was longing for uppers, downers, and alcohol to get through the day.

I was a nineteen-year-old piece of meat at home, raped by my first husband, and still not enough for him to keep from straying.

I was staring down the barrel of a gun, wondering if it might be better if this time the bullet hit.

I was in a mental hospital with no sense of reality.

I was abandoned.

I was a motherless mother feeling guilty for lost years.

I was dancing for older men in bars and restaurants.

I was an untouched wife, feeling worthless and unvalued.

I was powerless, lost, disconnected . . . bars down.

All of it came back in a kiss.

"No." I said. "We don't do that!" and I was done.

I was done with fifty-five years of pain and anguish.

I was done being okay with all of it.

When each awful, negative incident of my life was simply a part of history, I was able to just keep it behind me. I put each one on a page in a dusty old book that I never picked up to read. I wrote it off. I never absorbed or analyzed it. When it all came back that day, it wasn't one thing; it was everything. It swept over me in an overwhelming wave of loss and pain and anguish that suffocated and strangled.

I ceased being able to function.

At the time, I was involved in a quilting group, subconsciously always working to piece together the mismatched pieces of forgotten scraps — the continuing analogy for my own life. I decided I couldn't be around people and I wanted to let these women know that something happening in my life that kept me from returning to group, although I didn't know if I could ever truly explain just what it was that happened.

I pulled out stationery and a pen to write letters to the group. All my life, I had prized myself on my penmanship, but—as I wrote—my hand shook. I couldn't read my own writing and found I couldn't even sign my own name. I didn't want to write that name, the name that knew suffering.

Very few people knew of my history, but a couple of women who did, and who knew I had trouble dealing with the flood into my own past, told me I had to go to church.

I was, of course, born into what was, by description anyway, a Christian family. We were taken to church regularly and I guess I believed because that's just what I was raised to think, but God wasn't in my heart. When you're little, your parents make you go to church, and, when you get old enough to say "I ain't going!" you stop listening to anything that's being taught . . . even when you have to go, anyway.

So, decades later, I had no clue where to start back with God, or even if I wanted to do so.

Hadn't I been forgotten?

Abandoned?

For ten months, I continued numbly, going through the minimum to be considered still alive.

Work.

Eat.

Sleep.

GO.

And, eventually, that *GO*—for reasons I can't explain—led me through the doors of Fox River Christian Church, a large, nondenominational Christian church. I was welcomed warmly and sincerely.

> *"If any household or town refuses to welcome you or listen to your message, shake its dust from your feet as you leave."*
>
> *~Matthew 10:14 (NLT)*

It was Memorial Day weekend. There was a big military event with music and prayer and honor. I sat alone taking it all in and something broke. It was different than the day my uncle kissed my neck. That day, I froze. I stopped living. But, when I sat in church, covered by the prayers of strangers, listening to music that seemed to be written for me and a message that was spoken to me, it was the opposite.

I burst.

I started crying.

I wept away decades of tears.

I sobbed openly.

It was as though I had been drowning in my own suffering until that moment.

Something reached inside of me and pulled the plug on my old life. I had spent my years immersed in a tub of memories thick and filthy as polluted water. In a moment, that stifling filth just drained away from me and was replaced with the water of life.

Finally.

I could breathe.

I was cleaned.

My agony, my wounds, all of them washed away down the drain with my tears that day.

When I walked out of that church, and the light hit me outside, I was completely at peace. All of the things that had come back to me were simply . . . gone. I don't mean that I forgot them, but the emotion associated with them was wiped away. I knew I was where I had to be in that moment.

Memorial Day; maybe it was symbolic that I started my new life with a memorial to my old one.

Rose Lauchart

<u>All Five Bars Rockin'</u>
loved, wanted, driven, forgiven

I came so they can have real and eternal life, more and better life than they ever dreamed of.
        ~John 10:10 (MSG)

Rose Lauchart

The day after Dan died, the people of my new church family showed up for me in a big way. All of these people who I barely knew were at Dan's memorial service with food, offers of help, hugs, prayers, and affection. They came without need of invitation, or with expectation of something in return, but merely because they saw a need and chose to be the hands and feet to fill it. I was overwhelmed again, but this time, positively. My life was changing.

I look back at all the things I have been through in my life, I can see now how many times God has been by my side, the unwavering bar of presence in the middle of my hopelessness. He saved me from what could have been some really horrible outcomes.

He sent me animals when humans let me down.

He protected me behind brittle doors of broken down homes.

He restrained my father.

He kept the bullets from striking me.

He didn't give me the cold ability to take my own life or mutilate myself to a dangerous point.

He sobered me up.

He gave me a new community . . . the family I never had and the connections for which I'd always hoped.

Over time, as I have recognized God in my life, he has rebuilt the path toward total connection:

He gave me *attention*.

After that Valentine's Day dinner, in bible study a few days later, I'd felt ripped apart. I left there and said that He needed to bring things in my life. Shortly afterward, I started hearing God in little things. It was like I could hear him and see him in everything I did. I started paying attention. I heard Him in the things people said or did in my life.

He gave me *approval*.

When volunteering in the kitchen at my church, we pick on each other affectionately, in the sibling-like manner I'd always sought. I speak with my natural sass and brass; we greet with hugs. Every week, I get an awesome hug from my friend at church when they say, "greet someone". Then, we all go out to dinner together after cleaning the kitchen (Saturday night service; some of my Seventh Day Adventist habits die hard!)

He gave me *growth*.

I've become a better person. I give more and have more compassion. I also allowed myself to grow into my own gifts, my creativity and artistic endeavors.

He gave me *kindness*.

My church community is the family I never had. They are my sisters and brothers and, through them, I've also learned to find other connections, not to fear people, and not to fear being myself.

It strengthens my faith by knowing that God has had a purpose for me this whole time. Between the self-mutilation cries for help, to the times my life was threatened with guns and actually shot at it is only by God's Grace that I am alive.

The drugs and alcohol and looking for dance jobs could have all taken me down a path of complete destruction.

As every bar that connected me to humanity came crashing down, the bar that connected me to God grew so that, when I was done and I couldn't manage any longer, I didn't have to. That connection was powerful enough to give me Wi-fi to God with all five bars rockin'!

He gave me . . . GIVES me . . . *love*.

Most of all, God gave me an unexpected gift: forgiveness.

He didn't merely have the grace to forgive *my* mistakes, but he filled my heart so completely that the forgiveness overflowed from inside of me onto the people of my past. That book of my past wounds can never be rewritten, but with God's eyes, it can be reread to see new truths and reflect on the story with compassion and mercy.

❧ ❧

My forgiveness began with my uncle.

I went back to my uncle and told him, "You and I need to talk."

He said, "You need to understand what I've been through."

It was then that I found out about the role he had in my mom's side of the family.

He was the youngest, like Lee in my family, surrounded by other, older, abusers. I said, "I get it". His older brother had abused him. He had suffered, too.

I told him that what he did to me was inappropriate and not okay and he apologized. My words to him were the words I held inside for Allan, my father, the uncle who stayed at our house, when my brother was killed in Vietnam, my first husband. His apology covered all of them. He never leaned into his weakness again, with me or anybody else, for the rest of his days. When he died, it was as a beloved husband and community builder who had redeemed himself, and I had forgiven him.

I looked back at each of my abusers with my fresh eyes and saw *their* pains. I CHOSE forgiveness for each of them, one at a time.

I reflect with compassion for my mother who didn't know how to protect me; it must have been so hard for her.

I honor the momentary self-control my father had in the middle of a great weakness; how all-encompassing his shame must have been to keep him from acting.

I imagine a moment with Allan, standing tall in his Marine Corps blues, saluting a farewell that speaks remorse. I hope to see him in heaven, one day, free of the sickness of violence that kept him trapped in this world.

I pray that Bruce finds a life free of drug and alcohol dependence.

I remember my last moments with Dan and hold onto the peace we experienced in contrast to the cool contentment of our marriage.

For those still here in this world, my younger brother, my son, my first husband, I work at a connection with them, by tapping into the connection I have to God.

This gift of forgiveness may seem, on its surface, a generous and undeserved thing to bestow on those in my life who did me harm, but it is me for which it has truly been the gift. Forgiveness has freed me from the shackles of bitterness, fear, guilt, shame, and loss. When God emptied out the filth from my life, he didn't leave me empty. He filled me with a new light and left no room for things of the darkness.

"...Indeed, the water I give them will become in them a spring of water welling up to eternal life."

~John 4:14b (NIV)

❧

Through sexual abuse, self-doubt, verbal and mental abuse, and total neglect, I have been molded by God to go and help others find a new path in life. I hope and pray that by telling my story, it will help others make better choices in their lives and go find Jesus for the strength to do that.

The biggest thing that I want people to take from this is that they can have major boulders thrown on their paths of life, but if we allow God to be in control, He'll teach you a lesson through those obstacles. He's going to bring you to the other side, if you let Him. He can help you if you let Him.

Writing this book was not an easy thing to do, but God led me to it, so I am doing it and, compared to what my life was like before, this is a piece of cake. I turned my life completely over to Jesus and told him whatever He wanted in my life to bring it. With Jesus at my side, I have been so connected that I just let go and let God!

Ever since God and I connected, or — more accurately — since I recognized His presence, He has taken care of me and blessed me in more ways than I thought were possible.

He is in my heart.

He is in my soul.

He is in my life.

I am so high on the spiritual ladder, I can't even explain it. When I go to church, when I take communion, when I'm in Bible study, when I pray, I end up in tears, literally in tears, and people ask why I'm upset.

I say "God makes me emotional, for everything He's done for me."

He's my Rock, the one I count on all the time. I don't question Him. When He puts something there, I do it. God's got my back; I don't worry about it. A year ago, my shoulders and arms were numb because I think I was always told God is in control, but it never clicked; I hadn't felt it. When it did finally click, the numbness went away.

Looking back now, I don't know how I missed it.

God is my Savior; He has saved my life and I think that this book is part of the graduation day that I waited a lifetime to experience.

It was time for me to tell my story and here's where it continues . . . as a woman with Wi-Fi to God; All Five Bars Rockin'!

Rose Lauchart

This is my class picture in 1961. I am holding Billy, my guinea pig, who I trained to walk down the hall and turn the corner into my bedroom when I told him it was time for bed.

This poem is how God works in a nutshell. We don't just need faith, we need faith in <u>His</u> timeline as He is, after all, in charge of everything, even when we don't understand the reason or the timing.

There's a Reason

For ev'ry pain that we must bear
For ev'ry burden, ev'ry care,
There's a reason.
For ev'ry grief that bows the head,
For ev'ry teardrop that is shed,
There's a reason.
For ev'ry hurt, for ev'ry plight,
For ev'ry lonely, pain-racked night,
There's a reason.
But if we trust God, as we should,
It all will work out for our good,
He knows the Reason.

~Susan Conroy, Author
"Coming to Christ - Resting in His Love"

Rose Lauchart

Quilting in general has helped me keep my sanity, especially through all the years I spent with Dan, my now deceased husband, and all of his drama and crazy stuff.

This quilt was done for an art challenge. It is a windshield that is frosted over and then a hit-and-run on Frosty the Snowman.

Rose Lauchart

Acknowledgments

I want to thank Linda Jones who first took me to church.

God bless the Brookins (Brian and Annette), and the Dows (Randy and Ann) for leading a small group, inviting me in, and still including me to this day.

I'm grateful for the countless people God has surrounded me with in Bible Study and in the church kitchen. He keeps bringing me more and more fellow God Warriors.

I have gratitude for my uncle who, when I thought my life was fine, showed me how broken I still was. It was his act that led me to true healing.

I'm thankful to Dan for taking care of me.

To my publishing team – I have deep appreciation! Jessica who has been in this writing adventure with me, to Reji for her friendship and love, to Mike because "He got it!" and, to Angela who continues to work toward making sure that we can rock it all the way to five full bars.

I would like to make a special mention of Daystar, a non-profit organization that has been operating in Milwaukee, WI, for over thirty years. Daystar provides a safe haven for women survivors of Domestic Violence & Sexual Assault and empowers them to triumph over trauma and overcome barriers to leading successful, productive lives, free from violence.

Daystar's transformational and life-changing services go far beyond a 'band-aid' approach by providing safe housing, emotional healing and individualized counseling for up to two years. The program focuses on helping survivors develop the skills necessary to break the cycle of abuse.

I'm proud to support Daystar's mission.

I encourage you to visit their website: www.daystarinc.org.

I also would like to recognize Nancy Jo Baratti. Nancy Jo is a huge supporter, advocate, and donor to Daystar and their mission.

Nancy Jo is an Executive Senior Director with Mary Kay Cosmetics, and throughout the year she is constantly donating toiletries, clothes, paper products, as well as money to

Daystar. During the holidays, Nancy Jo and her Mary Kay Unit Consultants coordinate with their clients to donate Mary Kay shower gel, matching body lotion, and a Bilange sponge in a gift bag for each of the Daystar residents. Daystar is a home, and it is her mission to aid in making it *feel* like a home.

I am grateful to Nancy Jo for her work with Daystar.

Rose Lauchart

Resources

Are you seeking help for physical abuse, sexual abuse, drug addiction, or mental health issues? Here are a few places to turn:

National Sexual Assault Hotline
1-800-656-4673

National Domestic Violence Hotline
1-800-799-7233

National Suicide Prevention Lifeline
1-800-273-8255

National Substance Abuse Hotline
1-877-765-2164

Rose Lauchart

About Rose

Rose is a mostly self-taught entrepreneur with a heart of forgiveness and generosity. Having fun helping others fills her soul. Still the proud mother of a son who is now in his fifties, she embraced their older adult relationship that is growing and improving. She also has two teenaged grandkids she loves. A survivor of fibromyalgia, Rose is grateful to sell health and nutritional products through her company: **Be Fit Fuel**. *While she keeps busy quilting, volunteering at church and an antique store, landscaping, and working on her home, she looks forward to getting into the world to speak about abuse, God, and victory. She is anxious to speak about healing to women with low self-esteem, to former drug addicts, and to people who need a bigger hope. She wants to introduce God to their hearts and lives.*

Rose Lauchart

A Note from Rose's Co-author

*I'd like to start by thanking Jessica Sosnoski for her interviewing and initial outlining to help create this story. Typically, this is the part of the book when a co-author shares his or her bio - something that qualifies him or her to help create a person's book. Never before Rose's story have I ever felt so **UN**qualified to carry a person's life to pages, so I'm not doing that. Instead, I'd like to take this time to thank her for the honor and privilege of working with her. Rose is a woman like none I've ever met. Her heart of forgiveness is unmatched. She looks at her past abusers through the lens of Jesus and – in that choice – manages to see them with compassion instead of coldness. Often, when writing or editing Rose's tale, at times unbelievable in its darkness and depravity, I couldn't get through a single page . . . paragraph . . . sentence without breaking down and setting the work aside. I'd like to think Rose has experienced deep healing by sharing her life in these pages, but I know it is nothing compared to the deep inspiration she can provide to countless who have survived similar scenarios. As a biographer, I've learned the unfortunate truth that sexual abuse is far from rare. Recovery from it, though, is. In Rose, there is hope in the reality that joy after abuse is possible through Christ. It is my prayer that her message reaches victims around the world to turn them into victors over the tragedies of their pasts. God love ya', Rose, and so do I.   ~Reji*

Rose Lauchart

www.ingramcontent.com/pod-product-compliance
Lightning Source LLC
LaVergne TN
LVHW051247080426
835513LV00016B/1785